GW01007114

THE COST
OF OBEDIENCE

A STUDY IN JEREMIAH

BIBLE STUDIES TO IMPACT THE LIVES
OF ORDINARY PEOPLE

Christian Focus Publications

The Word Worldwide

Written by Dorothy Russell

PREFACE

GEARED FOR GROWTH

'Where there's LIFE there's GROWTH: Where there's GROWTH there's LIFE.'

WHY GROW a study group?

Because as we study the Bible and share together we can

- learn to combat loneliness, depression, staleness, frustration, and other problems
- get to understand and love each other
- become responsive to the Holy Spirit's dealing and obedient to God's Word

and that's GROWTH.

How do you GROW a study group?

- Just start by asking a friend to join you and then aim at expanding your group.
- Study the set portions daily (they are brief and easy: no catches).
- Meet once a week to discuss what you find.
- Befriend others, both Christians and non Christians, and work away together

see how it GROWS!

WHEN you GROW ...

This will happen at school, at home, at work, at play, in your youth group, your student fellowship, women's meetings, mid-week meetings, churches and communities,

you'll be REACHING THROUGH TEACHING

INTRODUCTORY STUDY

GOD'S MOUTHPIECE

Read Jeremiah 1:1-3, then take time to study this tree of the kings of Judah and become acquainted with their names.

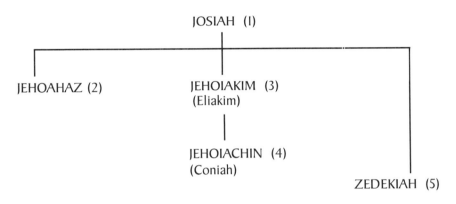

I. Josiah	2 Chronicles 34:1-2 2 Chronicles 35:22-24	639-609 BC
2. Jehoahaz	2 Chronicles 36:2-4	609 BC
3. Jehoiakim	2 Chronicles 36:5-6	608-597 BC
4. Jehoiachin	2 Chronicles 36:8-10	597 BC
5. Zedekiah	2 Chronicles 36:11-12	597-586 BC

Beside the name of each king, write the length of time he reigned.

* * *

Josiah and Jeremiah were born at about the same time, the darkest era in Israel's history. God was preparing a king who would endeavour to bring reform, and a prophet who would speak out His Word, as a last hope for a rebellious people.

At the age of 20, King Josiah began to purge his country of idolatry, and one year later Jeremiah received his call from God.

Read through Jeremiah 1:4-19. Then choose 2 people to read the parts of the Lord and Jeremiah, as in a play.

Discuss verse 5. Is the first half of the verse true for everyone? Or just true for every Christian? Or only a few? Is it true for you?

What were the testimonies of David (Ps. 139:16) and Paul (Gal. 1:15)?

For what service do you consider God has 'appointed' you?

How many times in verses 5, 7-10 and 17-19 do you find the word 'I' referring to God? Share your thoughts on the significance of what God says about Himself. How can you apply this to your own life?

Choose two different people and read the 'play' again.

How was Jeremiah like Moses in Exodus 4:10?

How was his experience like Isaiah's in Isaiah 6:7?

What did God do for him that He also did for Ezekiel in Ezekiel 3:3-4?

Look up the outworking of this in Jeremiah's life from Jeremiah 5:14; 15:16 and 20:9.

Why is it important for us to know God's word intimately?

Reread verses 10, 17-19. Put yourself in Jeremiah's shoes at this point. How would you feel? Why? What would be your only reassurance?

Missionaries today often testify that when things are really tough, the only reason they don't give up is that God clearly called them to that task in the first place, and He has not yet altered that call.

Spend a few minutes in quiet prayer, asking the Lord to show you how He wants you to serve Him. If you are not clear about this, keep asking Him each day for the next week. He has a purpose for each of us in this life and we need to know what it is. For Jeremiah it was to be GOD'S MOUTHPIECE. His call kept him going in the face of opposition and discouragement for over 40 years.

Selwyn Hughes has called the book of Jeremiah, 'one of the most powerful and spiritually productive books of the Old Testament'.

In our 10 week study it is not possible to cover every verse of the 52 chapters, hence the subtitle: 'A study in the life of Jeremiah'. Sometimes this requires reading a later chapter before an earlier one, to fit the story in chronologically (e.g. chs. 24 and 25).

Chapters 46-51 are not studied, as they contain oracles concerning other nations, and chapter 52 is a more detailed account of chapter 39.

STUDY 1

THE STATE OF THE NATION
(In the reign of King Josiah)

QUESTIONS

DAY 1 *Jeremiah 2:1-8,21.*
a) What two pictures are used to describe the original relationship between God and Israel?
b) Why was it unreasonable for the nation to forget God?

DAY 2 *Jeremiah 2:9-19.*
a) How was the nation suffering as a consequence of forsaking God?
b) Verse 13. Why is it never possible to forsake God and still find satisfaction?
What did Jesus say about living water in John 4:10, 14?

DAY 3 *Jeremiah 3:6-13.*
a) Who had refused to return (v. 7) and who was superficial in their return to the Lord (v. 10)?
b) On what condition were the people invited to return to the Lord again? How relevant is this condition for us today (1 John 1:9)?

DAY 4 *Jeremiah 3:21-4:4.*
a) What are the evidences of a genuine return to the Lord (vv. 23-25)?
b) What would it mean for the people to circumcise their hearts to the Lord (4:4)?

DAY 5 *Jeremiah 5:1-6.*
a) How widespread was the rebellion against God?
b) What does God look for in His people (v. 3; Ps. 51:6)?

DAY 6 *Jeremiah 5:26-31; 6:13-15.*
a) What important question were the people called upon to answer (5:31)? What is highlighted in Proverbs 16:25?
b) What were the prophets and priests particularly accused of (5:31; 6:13)? What particular form of deceit is mentioned in 6:14-15?

QUESTIONS (contd.)

DAY 7 *Jeremiah 6:16-19.*
a) What were the people encouraged to do? What would be the effect of doing this?
b) Where did Jesus say we would find rest for our souls (Matt. 11:28-29; John 14:6)?

NOTES

God pleads with His people
The first words the Lord gave Jeremiah to speak to the people were tender, pleading words, asking them to recall the time when He first called them to be His bride. God's plan was to create a family who loved Him and who would be faithful to Him.

What happened?
It almost seems as though God was bewildered about what had happened. What fault did they find in Him? Even the heathen nations do not change their gods, so how could His people forsake Him? He had done everything for them – how could they turn against Him? And the incredible thing was that they didn't even realise the depths of their sin. They said: 'We are not defiled by the Baals, we love foreign gods so we must go after them. We are free to do what we like – don't be angry with us!' The bride of long ago had become a prostitute.

Warnings of judgment
So what can God do? How can He pardon His people? They have not only forsaken Him, the spring of living water, but they have gone to broken cisterns which cannot give them what they need. Now He can only pronounce His judgments against them: a besieging army will come, they will devour the harvests and food, flocks and herds, sons and daughters, destroy cities with the sword, and lay waste the land.

BUT

God will not destroy His people completely. They will be led away to serve others in a strange land.

Is it any wonder that Jeremiah was unpopular with such a message to proclaim? We shall see as we continue with this study that everything the Lord told him at his call, came to pass. They would even fight against him. 'But,' said the Lord, 'they will not overcome you, for I am with you and will rescue you.'

STUDY 2
OBEDIENCE IS NUMBER ONE

QUESTIONS

DAY 1 *Jeremiah 7:1-7.*
a) Where was Jeremiah to deliver this message?
b) What were the people called upon to do?

DAY 2 *Jeremiah 7:8-11, 30.*
a) What is emphasised about the temple in verses 10, 11 and 30?
b) How did the people regard the temple?
c) Which verse did Jesus quote from in Matthew 21:12-13? Why might He have done this?

DAY 3 *Jeremiah 7:12-20; Joshua 18:1.*
a) What made Shiloh significant in Joshua's day?
b) What was going to happen to the temple?
c) Is God's anger (v. 20) just an Old Testament concept or has it a relevance for us today (John 3:36; 1 Thess. 1:10)?

DAY 4 *Jeremiah 7:21-8:3.*
a) What was particularly evil about the conduct of the people?
b) What should the people have been doing instead (v. 23; 1 Sam. 15:22)?

DAY 5 *Jeremiah 8:4-12.*
a) What false boast were the people making in verse 8?
b) How would those who thought they were wise be put to shame (v. 9)? What is said about wisdom in 1 Corinthians 1:18-25?

DAY 6 *2 Chronicles 34:14, 15, 29-33; Jeremiah 11:1-5.*
a) What does the 'Chronicles' reading tell us about the Book of the Covenant?
b) What did the Lord tell Jeremiah to do?

DAY 7 *Jeremiah 11:6-15.*
a) Where was Jeremiah's preaching tour to take him?
b) What were the people to learn from their past?
c) In spite of King Josiah's reforms, what was still happening? What was to be the consequence of this?

NOTES

The focal point of this week's study is in the words of chapter 7:22 and 23: 'I did not just give them commands about burnt offerings and sacrifices, but I gave them this command: OBEY ME'. The Ten Commandments give God's standard for right living, and the first one is 'You shall have no other gods besides me'.

It may be hard for us to understand how the people of Israel could burn incense to Baal, make cakes for the Queen of Heaven, and still claim God as their God, and worship at the temple! Yet there are people today who make other things their gods – e.g. sport, work, possessions – and still sit in church each Sunday and claim to be Christians. Let us search our own hearts to see if this could be true of us. Our Lord said: 'Not everyone who says to me, "Lord, Lord" will enter the kingdom of heaven, but only he who does the will of my Father who is in heaven.'

Putting other things in place of God leads to disregard of the other commandments, and the people of Jeremiah's day were guilty of stealing, murder, lying and adultery as well as not keeping the sabbath day holy (ch. 17).

GOD'S TACTICS:
1. His appeal to conscience: 'If you will do certain things, then I will let you live in this place'. Our longsuffering and patient God keeps His offer open, waiting for a response. The Bible is full of God's conditional promises, but we must obey the first part in order to claim the promise in the second.

> e.g. 'If my people ... will humble themselves and pray ... then will I forgive their sin and will heal their land' (2 Chron. 7:14).
> (If you) 'come to me ... I will give you rest' (Matt. 11:28).

2. His appeal to reason: 'Can't you see how unreasonable it is to steal, murder and commit adultery and then come to my house and say: "Now we are safe" – safe as robbers returning to their den where no one can catch them'?

Do we sometimes imagine God doesn't notice when we do things contrary to His Word? Remember that His eyes are 'open to all the ways of men' (Jer. 32:19) and He is 'watching' (7:11).

3. His appeal to history: 'What I did to Shiloh ...'

Don't imagine that God will not carry out His judgments on wickedness. The past experiences of the Israelites proved that He does not issue empty threats. Destruction will surely come to the beautiful temple built by Solomon, as it did to the tabernacle.

4. The finding of the book of the law: At the right time, and when Josiah had

instituted reforms to bring the people back to God, the book was found. Surely this would change their ways! They were now without excuse, the law was read and preached throughout the land, they were made to pledge themselves to keep the covenant ... and what happened?

'These people ... honour me with their lips,' said the Lord, 'but their hearts are far from me' (Isa. 29:13).

STUDY 3

QUESTIONS

(Read the Notes before you answer the questions this week.)

DAY 1 *Jeremiah 4:19-21; 8:21–9:2; Psalm 55:4-8.*
a) What caused Jeremiah to be full of anguish?
b) In their anguish, what did both Jeremiah and David long to do?

DAY 2 *Jeremiah 9:11-16, 23-24; Galatians 6:14.*
a) How did the Lord respond to the questions that plagued Jeremiah?
b) Which truth in these verses is again emphasised in 1 Corinthians 1:31?
c) What did Paul boast in?

DAY 3 *Jeremiah 10:1-16.*
a) Even in his depression, Jeremiah's spirits could be lifted by praising the Lord. What did he praise Him for?
b) How should we respond to this knowledge of God (v. 7)?

DAY 4 *Jeremiah 11:18-23.*
a) Why would Jeremiah have been particularly saddened by this threat on his life (compare v. 21 with Jer. 1:1 and 12:6)?
b) How can we, like Jeremiah, face difficult situations (v. 20)?

DAY 5 *Jeremiah 15:10, 15-21; chapter 1:18-19.*
a) What painful complaints does Jeremiah bring before the Lord?
b) What promise did God again give to him?

DAY 6 *Jeremiah 18:18-23; Nehemiah 4:4,5.*
a) What prayer did both Jeremiah and Nehemiah pray when they were provoked to the limit?
b) Matthew 5:43-44; 6:14; Luke 23:32-34. Why was the teaching and example of Jesus so revolutionary?

DAY 7 *Jeremiah 20:1-18.*
a) Why could Jeremiah not just give up being God's mouthpiece?
b) What truth continually sustained Jeremiah even in his most difficult moments (v. 11)?

NOTES

What did it cost Jeremiah to do the work God had assigned to him? In this study we catch glimpses, from several chapters, of the heart cry of the prophet to his God, and we look into his very soul.

In public, the words of God are on his lips as he proclaimed them to his fellow men, but in private the words of the man were poured out to God. It is in the secret place, as we commune with our Heavenly Father, that our hearts are 'laid bare before the eyes of him to whom we must give account' (Heb. 4:13). A man's prayers, more than anything else, reveal what he is really like.

Waves of depression overwhelmed Jeremiah from time to time, and we can see how his emotions were in turmoil. He loved his people and, as Isaiah said about God, 'In all their distress he too was distressed' (Isa. 63:9). Their suffering was his suffering, and yet they hated him. At times it became too much, and he cried out:

'Let me see your vengeance upon them' (11:20).
'Drag them off like sheep to be butchered' (12:3).

Perhaps we can identify with some of the depression and darkness that engulfed him. If so, it is important to notice how God dealt with His child at these times.

1. He understood him completely.
2. He gave him expressions of praise in the midst of his troubles.
3. He assured him that wickedness would not go unpunished.
4. He reminded him of his call to be the Lord's mouthpiece, and the promises made.
5. He said, in effect: 'Jeremiah, I'm depending on you. Trust me, and go on doing what I called you to do'.

When God chooses a person and calls him to do a specific task, we would expect that life would run smoothly. But this is not always the case, and the study of Jeremiah shows us that depression and things going wrong, are not marks of failure. Often they draw us close to God. Human nature cries out: 'Why is this happening? Why is my pain unending?' And God replies, 'Stay close to me, you are my child. Keep on serving me, that is what matters in life. I am with you'.

When one is down at the bottom of a pit, the only way to look is UP.

STUDY 4
PARABLES AND POTTERY

QUESTIONS

DAY 1 *Jeremiah 13:1-11.*
a) Why were Israel and Judah like the garment in this acted parable (see this week's notes)?
b) What relation exists between verse 11 and 1 Peter 2:9?
c) Are you fulfilling God's purpose as outlined in the New Testament reference?

DAY 2 *Jeremiah 17:5-8; Psalm 1.*
a) How is trust in man and trust in the Lord compared and contrasted?
b) To what is fruitfulness linked in Psalm 1?

DAY 3 *Jeremiah 17:9-18; John 2:24,25.*
a) How is the human heart described (v. 9)? What did Jesus say about the heart (Mark 7:20-23)?
b) How was Jeremiah's credibility being attacked (v. 15)? What do people scoff at today (2 Peter 3:3-7)?

DAY 4 *Jeremiah 17:19-27; Isaiah 58:13, 14.*
a) What did God expect His people to do?
b) How is the increasing commercialisation of Sunday harming our nation's spiritual health today?

DAY 5 *Jeremiah 18:1-12; Jonah 3:10; 1 Samuel 2:30-31.*
a) What did the potter do with the pot that was spoiled?
b) In what way is God like a potter?
c) Which verses in Jeremiah does the 'Jonah' reference illustrate? Which verses the 'Samuel' reference?

DAY 6 *Jeremiah 18:13-17; 2:10-13.*
a) How is the illustration from nature (v. 14) contrasted with the behaviour of the people?
b) What other illustration from nature is used to describe God's judgment on the nation?

QUESTIONS (contd.)

DAY 7 *Jeremiah 19:1-6, 10-15.*

a) How would the clay jar that Jeremiah bought be different from the one in chapter 18:4?

b) What was symbolised by the breaking of this jar?

c) What particularly evil practice of Baal worship is again denounced (v. 5)?

NOTES

Through Jeremiah, God has:

pleaded with His people,
  warned them of judgment,
    appealed for their obedience,
      had His law read throughout the land –

All to no avail.
What must He do to gain their attention?
He instructs Jeremiah to make His Word visible – to act out the message in ways of His choosing.

What was Jeremiah told to buy?
  a linen belt – NIV
  a loin cloth – LB
  a waistcloth (short kilt hugging the body) – RSV
  linen shorts – GNB

David Pawson calls it 'a pair of underpants'.
However the word is translated, certain things are important about this garment. It was new, fresh and clean, and its purpose was to cling closely to the body.

What was he told to do with it?
He was to wear it for a while, and then take it far away and hide it in a hole in the rocks by the river. After some time he was to go and dig it up.

The result?
A garment that had rotted and was ruined – totally useless for the purpose for which it was intended.

Another acted message from God – The Potter
Picture the scene in the potter's house: the pot he is working on is not turning out as he wishes, so what does he do? He, as it were, gives it another chance. He remakes the pot into the useful vessel he originally intended.

Then comes the explanation: if God pronounces doom on a nation or kingdom, and they repent – He can change His plan and fashion them into the kind of people He wants them to be. The converse is also true.

God's message through Jeremiah was this: 'I am warning of disaster and destruction for Judah, but there is still time to reverse this decision. Repent, and turn from your evil ways, and I can remake you'. Sadly, the reply in 18:12, indicates

JEREMIAH • STUDY 4 • PARABLES AND POTTERY • • • • •

15

that the people refused this offer.

This message from God is very important for us to understand. When a person repents and turns to God, God will reshape him, no matter what he was like beforehand. Just think of people like Peter, Saul of Tarsus, Matthew, or present-day examples. From being people who were not doing what they were created for, they became fit for the Master's use (2 Tim. 2:21).

Two ways are set out clearly before us: God's way, and man going his own way.

To get away from God, one doesn't have to commit terrible crimes; one simply has to forget about Him. Isn't that the problem with many in our world today? Make sure you don't fall into this trap.

The smashed jar
This dramatic visual aid was to be acted out in the presence of the elders and the priests; and probably a good many curious people witnessed it too.

Where was it performed?
Appropriately, at the gate of Broken Pottery, the rubbish dump close to the valley of Ben Hinnom, where children had been sacrificed by fire to Molech (Jer. 7:31).

What did Jeremiah have to do?
1) To proclaim that God would bring utter destruction on a nation who had forsaken Him and indulged in idolatrous practices.

2) He had to smash the jar to show what the nation would be like – beyond repair and useless to Him.

What happened next?
We read at the end of last week's references, that this drama made the priests so furious that they had Jeremiah beaten and put in the stocks overnight.

Jeremiah, the man who was 'useful' to the Lord, could expect only persecution from those who had turned against Him.

STUDY 5

A FEW FRIENDS
(In the reign of King Jehoiakim)

QUESTIONS

DAY 1 *2 Chronicles 34:1-2; 36:5.*
a) What kind of kings were Josiah and his son Jehoiakim?
b) Jeremiah 26:1-9. Who heard this message of Jeremiah from God? How did they react?

DAY 2 *Jeremiah 26:10-19, 24.*
a) Who, in this section, stood up for Jeremiah?
b) What can you find out about Ahikam from 2 Kings 22:8-13?

DAY 3 *Jeremiah 36:1-7.*
a) Who was Jeremiah's friend and secretary?
b) Why did the Lord want His words to Jeremiah written down?

DAY 4 *Jeremiah 36:8-15.*
a) How did Micaiah show that he feared the Lord?
b) To whom did Baruch read the words on the scroll the first time? And the second time?

DAY 5 *Jeremiah 36:16-26.*
a) Picture the scene in the winter palace. What did the king do?
b) How did his behaviour contrast with that of the king of Nineveh (Jonah 3:6-9)?
c) Who were the three officials who urged the king not to burn the scroll?

DAY 6 *Jeremiah 36:27-32.*
a) What punishment would come to Jehoiakim as a result of his action?
b) What task was Baruch entrusted with again?

DAY 7 *Jeremiah 45:1-5.*
a) How did Baruch feel after this great task?
b) What was God's message to him?

What a state the nation is in! In little more than three months they have lost good King Josiah killed in battle, seen his successor deported to Egypt, and now have on the throne an unscrupulous young man of twenty-five. (Look back to the family tree on page 3.)

What will God's message be to them at this unsettling time?

'If you do not listen to Me
I will utterly destroy the temple and the city.'

It was not the kind of message they wanted to hear and they made this quite clear to Jeremiah. Now he was threatened with death, but God had everything under control. He had His men there, even among the officials, to make good the promise He had given Jeremiah years before:

'They will fight against you
but will not overcome you,
for I am with you and will rescue you.'

SHAPHAN had been secretary to King Josiah, and was the man who read the book of the law when Hilkiah found it. He may have died by this time, but he had two sons:

1) AHIKAM who supported Jeremiah in the face of opposition,
2) GEMARIAH, one of the officials who prevented his murder.

Gemariah had a son MICAIAH, who also stood for what was right.

Ahikam had a son GEDALIAH, who, we shall see in Study 10, took Jeremiah under his wing until he himself was assassinated.

Praise the Lord for those who teach their children and grandchildren the faith that they themselves have! The godly example of parents is something we should never underestimate.

Now Jeremiah was restricted – no longer allowed to speak publicly. How could he continue to proclaim the message? God still had everything under control. He instructed Jeremiah to have all His words written down and read to the people.

BARUCH, a friend of Jeremiah, was a scribe, and he painstakingly wrote down all the messages we have been reading in this study.

The story of what the king did to that scroll is the first record of the Word of God being deliberately destroyed. Sadly, there have been many more attempts throughout history. Was God beaten at last? No, for He was still in control. He ordered Jeremiah and Baruch to start all over again.

Life is tough for our obedient prophet. Would you have gone on proclaiming God's Word in the face of such opposition? But God graciously gives him a few friends who will stand by him in his time of trouble.

Praise God, too, for people like Baruch, who do the difficult tasks, going the second mile, even if it means sacrificing their own welfare and position.

STUDY 6

GOD HAS HIS PLANS

QUESTIONS

DAY 1 *Jeremiah 25:1-11.*
a) How long had Jeremiah been speaking out God's word?
b) With what result?
c) What does God call Nebuchadnezzar in verse 9? Why is this?

DAY 2 *Jeremiah 25:12-14; 2 Chronicles 36:15-23; Ezra 1:1.*
a) What kingdom later came to power and overthrew Babylon, thus fulfilling verse 14?
b) What would happen to the land of Judah during these 70 years (2 Chron. 36:21)?
c) Pause for a moment to reflect on, and marvel at, the accurate fulfilment of God's prediction (Ezra 1:1).

DAY 3 *Jeremiah 24:1-5; Daniel 1:1-2.*
a) What disastrous event has occurred?
b) What group of people did God say were like good figs? Why?

DAY 4 *Jeremiah 24:6-10.*
a) What promises did the Lord give to the people in exile?
b) What group of people did the poor figs represent?

(In the reign of King Zedekiah)

DAY 5 *Jeremiah 29:1-9.*
a) Jeremiah remained in Jerusalem. To whom did he send this letter?
b) During their time of exile, what did God want His people to do? Why do you think He wanted them to do this?

DAY 6 *Jeremiah 29:10-14; Deuteronomy 4:29.*
a) How were these people, and how are we, to seek the Lord?
b) Which of the promises in these verses can apply to Christians today?

QUESTIONS (contd.)

DAY 7 *Jeremiah 29:24-32 (the letter Shemaiah wrote is in vv. 26-28).*

a) Describe the counter-attack on Jeremiah by Shemaiah.

b) What did Zephaniah do?

c) What was the Lord's reply through Jeremiah?

NOTES

In December 598 BC Jehoiakim was deposed and put in fetters to be deported to Babylon, but died at the outset of the journey. Jehoiachin his son barricaded Jerusalem against the Babylonians but surrendered after three months. He was taken into exile along with the cream of his citizens and the temple treasures. Nebuchadnezzar, the king of Babylon, then appointed a puppet king in Jerusalem, Zedekiah, uncle of Jehoiachin (see page 3).

If you had been there at that time, and had been among those allowed to stay in Jerusalem, you would have considered yourself very fortunate. How dreadful for the thousands who were carried away captive to Babylon! That would be the end of them, and it would seem that God was throwing them away like bad figs.

But, as so often happens, God's thoughts are not our thoughts, and nothing takes Him by surprise. He has His plans. His Word comes to Jeremiah: 'The exiles are the good figs, and those left in Jerusalem are the ones for whom there is no hope'.

How can this be?

Isn't God punishing them for their wickedness?

Yes, they certainly do not deserve God's favour, but this is a beautiful example of God's grace:

I sent them away.
My eyes will watch over them for their good.
I will give them a heart to know Me.
They will be My people and I will be their God.
My plans are to give them a hope and a future.

When difficult times or even tragedy comes into your life, think of this passage. Seek the Lord with all your heart and trust Him with your sorrows and problems. God has His plans for you, and He can bring something good out of the darkest days. He has not promised that there will be no hard times, but He has promised that He will be with you through those times, and that His eyes are always watching over you for good.

The fact that God put a limit of 70 years on the time of captivity reminds us that He knows the end from the beginning, and encourages us to hang on in times of distress, knowing that there will be light at the end of the tunnel.

STUDY 7
CONTRASTS

QUESTIONS

DAY 1 *Jeremiah 27:1-11.*
a) What strange thing did the Lord ask Jeremiah to do?
b) What was the message for the nations of Edom, Moab, etc.?

DAY 2 *Jeremiah 27:12-22.*
a) What was the message to King Zedekiah?
b) What does God say will happen to the treasures that remain in Jerusalem (Ezra 1:7, 11)?

DAY 3 *Jeremiah 28:1-17.*
a) How did the false prophet Hananiah illustrate his message?
b) How did Jeremiah react? How is a true prophet recognised?

DAY 4 *Jeremiah 37:1-10.*
a) What do verses 2 and 3 tell us about Zedekiah?
b) What did God say would happen regarding the two most powerful nations of that day?

DAY 5 *Jeremiah 37:11-21.*
a) Why was Jeremiah arrested and imprisioned?
b) What request did Jeremiah make to the king?

DAY 6 *Jeremiah 38:1-13; Psalm 69:1-2, 14-19.*
a) What impresses you most about Ebed-Melech's action?
b) Why might Jeremiah have thought of this psalm in his distress?

DAY 7 *Jeremiah 38:14-28; 2 Chronicles 36:11-13.*
a) What have you discovered about Zedekiah from this week's readings?
b) What have you discovered so far about Jeremiah?

TRUE AND FALSE

The true prophet

The greatest world power of the day was Babylon. Already Nebuchadnezzar had attacked Jerusalem once and was likely to do so again. What was to be done? Zedekiah summoned envoys from Edom, Moab, and Ammon in the South, and Tyre and Sidon in the North to plan a strategy for defence, through an Eastern Mediterranean alliance. How far they got with their discussions, we don't know. But in walked the prophet Jeremiah with an ungainly yoke used for animals around his neck. There is no doubt that this would instantly attract their attention!

His message:

1) The Creator God, the God of Israel, is Sovereign and will give the nations of the earth to anyone He pleases.
2) Nebuchadnezzar, the greatest power on earth, is merely a servant of the Almighty.
3) God's plan is for all nations to be subject to Nebuchadnezzar for a time.
4) So bow your neck under his yoke, which in fact is God's yoke too.

It's not hard to imagine the kind of reception Jeremiah got as he delivered his message, not only to the envoys, but later to the king, the priests and all the people.

The false prophet

His message, also delivered in a dramatic way as he took off Jeremiah's yoke and broke it, was:

1) Within 3 years Babylon's power will be broken.
2) The temple treasures will be restored.
3) Jehoiachin and all the exiles will return.

But this prophet only lived for another 2 months, not long enough to see that none of his prophecies came true.

FEAR AND FAITH

Zedekiah and Jeremiah each had a measure of FAITH, and both had reason to FEAR.

Zedekiah's FEARS, however, overcame the little FAITH he had.
Jeremiah's FAITH, on the other hand, gave him power to overcome his FEARS.

Which one are you like?

Zedekiah – believed in theory that prayer was important.
         – was not willing to accept God's Word to him.
         – was afraid of the Babylonians and the Jews who had gone over to
           them.

Jeremiah – knew that prayer was vital, and prayed continually.
         – accepted a difficult assignment and spoke out God's Word
           faithfully.
         – feared God, and trusted his life to Him.

A wise man said, 'If you fear God, you will fear no-one else'.

STUDY 8

THE NEW COVENANT

QUESTIONS

Read chapters 30 and 31 at home during the week, as background to this week's study.

DAY 1 *Jeremiah 30:1-15.*
a) What promise is made concerning the future of Judah and Israel?
b) How does God tenderly explain the reason behind their suffering (vv. 11, 14, 15)?
c) What was to be unique about Israel (v. 11)?

DAY 2 *Jeremiah 31:31-32.*
a) What stipulations and promises were included in the old covenant (Exod. 19:3-6)?
b) Did the people agree to the terms of this covenant (Exod. 24:3-8)?

DAY 3 *Exodus 32:7-8; Jeremiah 11:1-10.*
a) What had the people consistently done from the time of Moses to Jeremiah's day?
b) What does this behaviour tell us about the old covenant?

DAY 4 *Jeremiah 31:33-34; Ezekiel 36:25-27.*
a) What four features of the new covenant does Jeremiah give?
b) How does Ezekiel describe it?

DAY 5 *Exodus 24:8; Matthew 26:27-28; Hebrews 9:18-22.*
a) How were both the old and new covenants inaugurated?
b) What did the Lord Jesus associate with the new covenant (Matt. 26:28)?

DAY 6 *Luke 22:20; Hebrews 8:6-13; 10:11-18.*
a) What is the significance of calling this the 'new' covenant?
b) What does God mean by saying that He would put His laws in their minds and write them on their hearts?

DAY 7 *Jeremiah 31:35-37.*
a) How does God illustrate His might from nature?
b) Why does He use these illustrations from nature?

NOTES

Some have said that the revelation of the new covenant given to Jeremiah is not only the mountain top of Jeremiah's experience, but also the high peak of the whole Old Testament.

Just imagine the extraordinary situation. Jeremiah is imprisoned in the courtyard of the guard, famine and plague rage in the city, and the army of Babylon is battering against the walls of Jerusalem. This is Judah's midnight hour – what hope can there be for her?

Although there is nothing by which to date chapters 30 and 31, it is believed that Jeremiah received this vision at this time. It is a vision of HOPE; first, for the return of the exiles to their own land; second, for the bringing in of a new covenant and third, for the time when all God's people will know Him fully and intimately.

Why did God promise a NEW covenant?

Clearly, because there was something wrong with the OLD covenant.

The Old	The New
The laws were external	God would write these laws on their hearts.
Breaking this brought a curse.	Keeping this brings forgiveness and freedom.
The motivation for keeping it was duty.	Motivation – people knew and loved God.
It proved impossible to fulfil.	The Holy Spirit would enable people to keep it.
It was for the Jews only.	For the world – 'everyone who believes'.
Ratified by shedding blood of animals.	Jesus' death ushered in the new.
Animal sacrifices over and over again could never take away sins.	Sins are forgiven by Jesus' sacrifice once and for all.

The old covenant, the book of the law, was rediscovered in Jeremiah's day, but the response by the people was short-lived, and died with the death of King Josiah.

The new covenant is an everlasting covenant. God will inspire His people to love and fear Him so that they will never turn away from Him.

Do you have God's law in your mind, written on your heart? Have you an intimate, personal relationship with Him? Then, as you know He has forgiven your sins and will remember them no more, you can have hope, as Jeremiah did. Whatever happens in this life, you can know with assurance that when you leave it you will be with your Lord for all eternity.

STUDY 9

GOD'S PROMISES DO NOT FAIL

QUESTIONS

DAY 1 *Jeremiah 32:1-15; Hebrews 11:1.*
a) Why did Jeremiah agree to buy the field which at that time was occupied by the Babylonians? What do you think others felt about this?
b) What had God promised in chapter 29:10?

DAY 2 *Jeremiah 32:16-25.*
In which verses does Jeremiah focus on:
a) the creative power of God?
b) His faithfulness and justice?
c) His redemptive acts?
d) the people's failure?
e) present difficulties?
f) the mystery of God's plan?
Perhaps we can learn from this how to pray in times of difficulty.

DAY 3 *Jeremiah 32:26-35; Genesis 18:13-14; Matthew 19:26.*
a) What is the only answer possible to the question in verse 27? Do you believe this?
b) Then why did God not save Jerusalem from the enemy?

DAY 4 *Jeremiah 32:36-44.*
a) Pick out two exciting promises that apply to Christians today.
b) What special promise did God give to Jeremiah, to encourage him that he had done the right thing?

DAY 5 *Jeremiah 33:1-3; Isaiah 58:9; 65:24.*
a) There is a lovely promise in verse 3. Learn it by heart and ponder it during the week.
b) Share some examples of how you have found this to be true.

DAY 6 *Jeremiah 34:1-7; 27:12-13; 38:17-18, 28.*
a) What message did God repeatedly give to Zedekiah through Jeremiah?

QUESTIONS (contd.)

b) Read Jeremiah 39:6-7 to see how this came to pass. What had God, in His mercy, concealed from Zedekiah beforehand?

DAY 7 *2 Peter 1:3, 4; Proverbs 3:5-6; Matthew 6:14, 33; John 14:2-3. 1 Corinthians 10:13.*
Here are a few of God's promises. Can you think of any more? Which one do you claim most often?

NOTES

When you read God's promises, do you get a 'warm fuzzy' feeling? How wonderful that His promises never fail!

But wait ... Have you noticed that there is a condition to be fulfilled when a promise is given?

'Trust in the Lord	...	and he will make your paths straight.'
'If you forgive men	...	your heavenly Father will forgive you.'
'Seek first his kingdom	...	and all these things will be given to you.'
'Call to me	...	and I will answer you.'

God said to Zedekiah : 'If you surrender ... your life will be spared'.
And to the people of Judah : 'Ask where the good way is, and walk in it ... and you will find rest'.

So we have a choice. If we want what God has promised, we must fulfil the condition. Zedekiah wanted to be spared, but he was not prepared to surrender. The people of Judah wanted rest, but they did not want to go God's way.

* * *

But God does not only promise good things, He promises punishment and rejection for those who will not turn to Him.

To the people He said (Jer. 27:8): 'If ... any nation ... will not serve Nebuchadnezzar ... I will punish that nation'.

And to Zedekiah (Jer. 38:18): 'If you will not surrender ... you ... will not escape'.

He says to us :
'If you do not forgive men ... your Father will not forgive your sins' (Matt. 6:15).
'If you do not obey the LORD ... his hand will be against you' (I Sam. 12:15).
'If anyone takes words away from this book ... God will take away from him his share ... in the holy city' (Rev. 22:18).
'If any nation does not listen, I will ... uproot and destroy it' (Jer. 12:17).

Remember, God's promises do not fail. 'God is not a man, that he should lie' (Num. 23:19).

STUDY 10

HOW DID IT ALL END?

QUESTIONS

DAY 1 *Jeremiah 39:1-10; Lamentations 1:1-3.*
a) What was Zedekiah's fate?
b) How does Jeremiah describe Jerusalem in his 'Lamentations' poem?

DAY 2 *Jeremiah 39:11-18; 38:12-13.*
a) What happened to Jeremiah?
b) What reason did God give for rescuing Ebed-Melech?

DAY 3 *Jeremiah 40:1-6.*
a) What choice did Jeremiah have?
b) What do you remember about Ahikam, father of Gedeliah? (STUDY 5, DAY 2)

DAY 4 *Jeremiah 41:1-3,16-18; 42:1-6.*
a) What happened to Gedaliah?
b) What request, and what promise did the army officers make to Jeremiah?

DAY 5 *Jeremiah 42:7-22; 43:1-7 (read to v. 13 at home).*
a) What was the Lord's answer? Does the reaction of the officers sound familiar?
b) Where did they go? Who did they take with them?

DAY 6 *Jeremiah 44:1-8, 15-18, 24-28.*
a) What evil did the people persist in, even after God's punishment? Remember God's word in 24:8? What were the people like?
b) What would the remnant who went to Egypt eventually find out?

DAY 7 *Jeremiah 46:27-28; 51:5; Lamentations 3:19-26.*
a) Though Jeremiah had a sad life, he had one tremendous consolation. What was it?
b) In the midst of any trial, what should we do?

NOTES

This has been a study in the life of Jeremiah, so let's keep him in focus as we read the narrative of what happened after the fall of Jerusalem.

1. Jeremiah is released from the courtyard of the guard and given his freedom among the people.
2. He is mistakenly rounded up and put in chains along with the people being taken to Babylon.
3. Nebuzaradan finds him and releases him, giving him the choice of doing whatever he likes. He stays with Gedeliah.
4. Gedeliah is assassinated, and the people ask Jeremiah to pray to the Lord to direct them. He is silent for 10 days.
5. Finally, he gives the word from the Lord: 'Do not go to Egypt'. However, they disobey, and take Jeremiah with them.
6. Some months, or even years pass, and the people settle in Egypt in places far apart. (44:1).
7. One last time, God gives Jeremiah a word – a rebuke for all the people in their idolatrous ways. One can almost hear the sob in the prophet's voice as he delivers it.

This reminds us of the words of Jesus in Matthew 23:37: 'O Jerusalem, Jerusalem ... how often I have longed to gather your children together, as a hen gathers her chicks under her wings, but you were not willing'.

For Jeremiah, there was a high cost of obedience to God. He is sometimes called 'the weeping prophet'. For many people even today, it is costly to follow Christ, and may mean persecution, imprisonment, being cast out of one's family, or even killed. Yet the Bible tells us that these 'were all commended for their faith', and 'there is in store for (them) the crown of righteousness which the Lord, the righteous Judge, will award to (them) on that day' (Heb. 11:39 and 2 Tim. 4:8).

May Jeremiah be an inspiration to us, to walk in the good way whatever the cost.

ANSWER GUIDE

The following pages contain an Answer Guide. It is recommended that answers to the questions be attempted before turning to this guide. It is only a guide and the answers given should not be treated as exhaustive.

GUIDE TO INTRODUCTORY STUDY

Be well acquainted with the order of the five kings who reigned in Judah during Jeremiah's prophetic life, as they will be important throughout the study. Encourage your group members to become familiar with their names. Choose good readers to read the parts in the play, as this will make it come alive, and try to stimulate discussion on the personal questions.

Much of the enthusiasm for this study will depend on you, the leader, as you may find your group members do not know this book well.

GUIDE TO STUDY 1

DAY 1
a) As a bride showing devotion and as a vineyard bearing good fruit.
b) They had been totally dependent on God. God had showered rich blessings on them including giving them the land they were now in.

DAY 2
a) It was being devastated by invaders.
b) God is the only 'spring' that gives living water, not just a cistern that catches water if it rains and even then cannot retain it.
Jesus alone is the living water that gives eternal satisfaction.

DAY 3
a) The northern kingdom, Israel, which had already gone into captivity.
The southern kingdom, Judah. This probably refers to the effect of Josiah's reforms detailed in 2 Chronicles 34, 35.
b) They were to acknowledge their guilt and rebellion against the Lord.
Confession of sin is always a prerequisite to forgiveness.

DAY 4
a) An acknowledgement of the worthlessness and shame of a sinful life, a confession of sin, a changed life (here the putting away of their idols).
b) Cut out the evil that was there by nature and love the Lord with all their hearts.

DAY 5
a) All sections of the people were included in it, from the poor to the leaders.
b) Truth.

DAY 6
a) They were to ponder what would happen in the end, to consider the consequences of their disobedience.
A way that may appear right to us could end in eternal death.
b) Of telling lies and deceiving the people.
They did not realise the serious situation the nation was in. They condoned the sin of the people instead of challenging it.

DAY 7
a) They were to seek out the 'good way' (NIV) and walk in it. They would find rest for their souls.
b) In coming to Himself. He is also the Way.

GUIDE TO STUDY 2

DAY 1 a) At the gate of the temple.
b) To radically alter their moral and religious behaviour.

DAY 2 a) It is God's house as it bears His Name.
b) They saw it as inviolate, a place of safety which God would never let be destroyed. To them the building was more important than the Divine Presence of which it was the symbol.
c) Verse 11. Those buying and selling were acting dishonestly, contrary to the purpose for which the temple was built.

DAY 3 a) The Tabernacle, or Tent of Meeting, was set up there. It remained there until the events of I Samuel 4:10-11.
b) It was also going to be destroyed.
c) To live rejecting God is still to be under His wrath, even today. Jesus died to save us from this wrath and bring us into fellowship with God (Rom. 5:9).

DAY 4 a) Offering their sons and daughters as human sacrifices.
b) Obeying the Lord.

DAY 5 a) They imagined they were wise simply because they had the law. Their leaders were guilty of falsely interpreting it which would have disastrous consequences.
b) Their prophecies would never be fulfilled (e.g. as referred to above, the temple would be destroyed). They would be punished (v. 12).
God's wisdom is seen in that only the preaching of the cross results in salvation. History shows that human solutions to man's need are failures.

DAY 6 a) It (the first 5 books of the Bible) was discovered when the temple was being repaired. Josiah read it to the people and made them pledge themselves to it.
b) Keep on telling the people about the covenant and urge them to obey it.

DAY 7 a) To all the towns in Judah as well as Jerusalem.
b) That failure to obey the covenant brings judgment.
c) They were still committing the sins of their fathers and following other gods, that is, their hearts were unchanged.
Judgment would be inevitable and unavoidable.

GUIDE TO STUDY 3

DAY 1 a) His insight into the terrible suffering the people would endure as a result of their disobedience.
b) Jeremiah and David both wished to get right away to the desert.

DAY 2 a) God emphasised that His judgment must fall on those who persistently disobey Him.
b) Our boasting is to be only in the Lord. (Note that we are not to boast about our own achievements.)
c) In the cross of the Lord Jesus Christ.

DAY 3 a) His uniqueness, His greatness, His creation of the heavens and the earth, etc.
b) With reverence and worship.

DAY 4 a) It came from members of his own family.
b) By not seeking personal revenge and instead committing our situation to the Lord.

DAY 5 a) He has done nothing wrong, yet everyone was cursing him. He had great joy in proclaiming God's Word yet had to endure loneliness and endless suffering.
b) God again promised to be with him and deliver him.

DAY 6 a) They asked God not to forgive the crimes or blot out the sins of those who were their enemies.
b) Because no-one had ever thought of loving and forgiving their enemies as it appeared so unnatural.

DAY 7 a) God's word burned in his heart like a fire and he couldn't hold it in.
b) The knowledge that God was still with him.

GUIDE TO STUDY 4

DAY 1　　a) God chose the nation to be His special possession, to cling closely to Him, to be clean and pure. But they had committed themselves instead to a far-off heathen power, and as a result had become useless to the Lord, their spiritual fibre rotten.
b) God's people in any generation are to be a witness to His grace and glory. People should see what God is like in what He has done for believers.
c) Personal.

DAY 2　　a) Compared to a bush and a tree. The bush has limited prospects because of its hostile environment while the tree is always fruitful as its roots have a constant source of water.
b) To a separation from evil and constant meditation on God's Word.

DAY 3　　a) As very deceitful with no natural cure.
It is the source of all evil. The heart of the problem is the problem of the heart!
b) They wouldn't believe he was speaking out God's Word unless it was actually fulfilled before their very eyes.
The coming again of the Lord Jesus.

DAY 4　　a) To strictly keep the sabbath day holy.
b) Personal. Suggestions perhaps could include: people are becoming more materialistic; there is a temptation to neglect church attendance; some are obliged to work who otherwise would not have wanted to; family life can suffer; people are not resting as they should with a resulting increase in stress-related illnesses, etc.

DAY 5　　a) He remade it to be the kind of pot he wanted.
b) God, like a potter, does what pleases Himself. If a nation repents He is not obliged to punish it and, vice-versa, if a nation persistently sins, He is not bound by past promises to do good to it.
c) Verses 7 and 8. Verses 9 and 10.

DAY 6　　a) The people's behaviour towards God had changed while the phenomena in verse 14 continued to exist.
b) They would be scattered as chaff or dust before an easterly wind.

DAY 7　　a) It would have been hardened and fired and could not be reshaped.
b) It symbolised the sentence of doom passed on the nation.
c) Human sacrifices.

GUIDE TO STUDY 5

DAY 1
a) Josiah: a righteous, God-fearing king.
Jehoiakim: an evil king.
b) The priests, prophets and all who came to worship.
They mobbed and threatened to kill him.

DAY 2
a) The officials and Ahikam son of Shaphan.
b) His father was secretary to King Josiah. When the Book of the Law was found, Ahikam was the man the king asked to enquire of the Lord about what had been read.

DAY 3
a) Baruch.
b) So that they could be read to the people even though Jeremiah was restricted and couldn't go to the temple. Also, so that we can read them too.

DAY 4
a) He went to the officials and told them what he had heard, indicating that he knew it was true.
b) First, to all the people who had gathered at the temple; then to the officials.

DAY 5
a) He cut up the scroll as it was read, section by section, and burned it.
b) The king of Nineveh repented and proclaimed a fast on hearing of God's judgment.
c) Elnathan, Delaiah and Gemariah.

DAY 6
a) No descendants of his would sit on the throne and his body would be thrown out when he died.
b) To write down again everything that Jeremiah dictated.

DAY 7
a) He was exhausted and discouraged.
b) He was to be satisfied that his life would be spared despite the coming disaster on the nation.

GUIDE TO STUDY 6

DAY 1
a) 23 years.
b) The people wouldn't listen.
c) My servant. Because, although he did not worship God, God used him to accomplish His will.

DAY 2
a) Persia.
b) It would enjoy its sabbath rests (Exod. 23:10, 11).
c) Personal.

DAY 3
a) Nebuchadnezzar has carried off captive most of the people of Israel.
b) Those exiles who had been taken to Babylon. Because they would eventually return to Him with all their heart.

DAY 4
a) That He would watch over them, bring them back to their own land, and give them a heart to know Him as their God.
b) The people who had been left in Jerusalem with Zedekiah, or who went to live in Egypt.

DAY 5
a) To the exiles in Babylon.
b) To settle down in the land of their captivity, marry and have children, and pray for the city where they were.
To encourage them to be content and to enjoy a peaceful life until God's time should come for them to return.

DAY 6
a) With all their (our) hearts.
b) Discussion. Verses 11–13. The Christian's bright future is found in I Thessalonians 5:9-10. Answers to prayers are found in Matthew 7:7-11.

DAY 7
a) He sent letters to the priests and people in Jerusalem claiming that Jeremiah was a false prophet.
b) He read the letter to Jeremiah.
c) The Lord's message was that He had not spoken through Shemaiah, and He would punish him and his descendants.

GUIDE TO STUDY 7

DAY 1
a) Make a yoke and put it on his neck. (If you can, bring a picture of animals yoked together, or explain it to your group.)
b) God is Sovereign (note v. 5) and is going to hand over all these countries to Babylon, therefore submit to Nebuchadnezzar for a time.

DAY 2
a) The same as for the other nations.
b) They will be taken to Babylon and remain there until the Lord brings them back.

DAY 3
a) He took the yoke off Jeremiah's neck and broke it.
b) Very calmly! He walked away and did not retaliate, or even speak until the Lord told him to.
His predictions come true.

DAY 4
a) He paid no attention to the words of the Lord, yet at a time of crisis he asked Jeremiah to pray for him.
b) The Egyptian army, which had come to support Judah, would return home, and then the Babylonians would capture Jerusalem and burn it down.

DAY 5
a) He was accused of deserting to the Babylonians.
b) That he would not be sent back to the dungeon in the house of Jonathan.

DAY 6
a) Personal.
b) Because it described his situation literally although the writer may have written it metaphorically.

DAY 7
a) Personal discoveries – e.g. he was weak, fearful, ungodly, unwilling to follow God's advice.
b) He was strong in faith, willing to speak out God's Word even if it cost him his life; sad at the future prospects for his people.

GUIDE TO STUDY 8

DAY 1   a) They would return to possess their own lands.
b) He had to discipline and punish them for their many sins.
c) It was never to be completely destroyed.

DAY 2   a) The people were to fully obey God, and God would make them His special people.
b) Yes. They said they would do everything the Lord had said.

DAY 3   a) Broken God's covenant.
b) It failed because the people could not keep it.

DAY 4   a) 1) God would put his law in their hearts; 2) He would be their God; 3) the people would know Him; 4) God would forgive their sin.
b) God will remove their heart of stone and give them a heart of flesh, and will put His Spirit in them.

DAY 5   a) With the shedding of blood.
b) The forgiveness of sins.

DAY 6   a) It implies that the old one has been superseded.
b) Those whose sins are forgiven have an inner desire to keep God's laws, rather than trying to obey them out of a sense of duty.

DAY 7   a) All aspects of nature are under His control, such as the sun, moon and stars, the sea and waves.
b) To demonstrate that He was able to fulfil the obligations that He had undertaken on behalf of His people.

GUIDE TO STUDY 9

DAY 1 a) He knew that God was telling him to buy it; He had faith that one day his people would return.
That he was extremely foolish.
b) After 70 years God would bring His people back.

DAY 2 a) Verse 17
b) Verse 18
c) Verses 20-22
d) Verse 23
e) Verse 24
f) Verse 25

DAY 3 a) There is nothing to hard for the Lord. Personal.
b) It was God's plan to punish them for their wickedness, and in fact He says He is handing them over to the Babylonians.

DAY 4 a) God is their God and they are His people.
God has made an everlasting covenant with them (see Study 8).
b) That fields would once again be bought for silver, and deeds signed, sealed and witnessed.

DAY 5 a) Personal.
b) Personal.

DAY 6 a) If he refused to surrender to the King of Babylon, he would be captured and the city devastated.
b) That Nebuchadnezzar would slay his sons before his eyes, then put out his eyes before taking him away. Note that God stressed that Zedekiah would see Nebuchadnezzar with his own eyes.

DAY 7 Personal.

GUIDE TO STUDY 10

DAY 1 a) To have his sons killed before his eyes.
To be blinded and shackled and led away to Babylon.
b) As a lady who was a queen but has become a slave.

DAY 2 a) Nebuchadnezzar gave orders that he was not to be harmed but freed, and whatever he wanted was to be done for him.
b) Because Ebed-Melech trusted in God. Note that nothing is said of his heroism or compassion, only his faith in God.

DAY 3 a) LB translates verse 4: '... If you want to come with me to Babylon, fine; I will see that you are well cared for. But if you don't want to come, don't. The world is before you – go where you like.'
b) He had been secretary to King Josiah when the book of the law was found and had helped prevent Jeremiah from being put to death.

DAY 4 a) He was murdered.
b) They requested that Jeremiah pray to the Lord God to find out where and what they were to do.
They promised to obey whatever answer they received.

DAY 5 a) Do not go to Egypt. They were continuing to reject God's Word coming through His prophet Jeremiah.
b) To Egypt. All those who remained with Gedeliah, including Jeremiah and Baruch.

DAY 6 a) Worshipping other gods, especially the Queen of Heaven.
They were like bad figs.
b) They would find out that God's Word would stand firm – not theirs.

DAY 7 a) God, because of His great love and compassion, would never forget His own people.
b) Wait quietly for the Lord and His salvation.

NOTES

NOTES

THE WORD WORLDWIDE

We first heard of WORD WORLDWIDE over 20 years ago when Marie Dinnen, its founder, shared excitedly about the wonderful way ministry to one needy woman had exploded to touch many lives. It was great to see the Word of God being made central in the lives of thousands of men and women, then to witness the life-changing results of them applying the Word to their circumstances. Over the years the vision for WORD WORLDWIDE has not dimmed in the hearts of those who are involved in this ministry. God is still at work through His Word and in today's self-seeking society, the Word is even more relevant to those who desire true meaning and purpose in life. WORD WORLDWIDE is a ministry of WEC International, an interdenominational missionary society, whose sole purpose is to see Christ known, loved and worshipped by all, particularly those who have yet to hear of His wonderful name. This ministry is a vital part of our work and we warmly recommend the WORD WORLDWIDE 'Geared for Growth' Bible studies to you. We know that as you study His Word you will be enriched in your personal walk with Christ. It is our hope that as you are blessed through these studies, you will find opportunities to help others discover a personal relationship with Jesus. As a mission we would encourage you to work with us to make Christ known to the ends of the earth.

Stewart and Jean Moulds – British Directors, **WEC International**.

A full list of over 50 'Geared for Growth' studies can be obtained from:

ENGLAND   John and Ann Edwards
5 Louvain Terrace, Hetton-le-Hole, Tyne & Wear, DH5 9PP
Tel. 0191 5262803 Email: rhysjohn.edwards@virgin.net

IRELAND   Steffney Preston
33 Harcourts Hill, Portadown, Craigavon, N. Ireland, BT62 3RE
Tel. 028 3833 7844 Email: sa.preston@talk21.com

SCOTLAND Margaret Halliday
10 Douglas Drive, Newton Mearns, Glasgow, G77 6HR
Tel. 0141 639 8695 Email: m.halliday@ntlworld.com

WALES   William and Eirian Edwards
Penlan Uchaf, Carmarthen Road, Kidwelly, Carms., SA17 5AF
Tel. 01554 890423 Email: Penlan.uchaf@farming.co.uk

UK CO-ORDINATOR
Anne Jenkins
2 Windermere Road, Carnforth, Lancs., LA5 9AR
Tel. 01524 734797 Email: anne@jenkins.abelgratis.com

UK Website: www.wordworldwide.org.uk

Christian Focus Publications

publishes books for all ages

Our mission statement –

STAYING FAITHFUL

In dependence upon God we seek to help make His infallible word, the Bible, relevant. Our aim is to ensure that the Lord Jesus Christ is presented as the only hope to obtain forgiveness of sin, live a useful life and look forward to heaven with Him.

REACHING OUT

Christ's last command requires us to reach out to our world with His gospel. We seek to help fulfill that by publishing books that point people towards Jesus and help them to develop a Christ-like maturity. We aim to equip all levels of readers for life, work, ministry and mission.

Books in our adult range are published in three imprints.

Christian Focus contains popular works including biographies, commentaries, basic doctrine, and Christian living. Our children's books are also published in this imprint.

Mentor focuses on books written at a level suitable for Bible College and seminary students, pastors, and other serious readers; the imprint includes commentaries, doctrinal studies, examination of current issues, and church history.

Christian Heritage contains classic writings from the past.

For details of our titles visit us on our website
www.christianfocus.com

ISBN 0 908067 61 5

Copyright © WEC International

Published in 2002 by
Christian Focus Publications, Geanies House,
Fearn, Ross-shire, IV20 ITW, Scotland
and
WEC International, Bulstrode, Oxford Road,
Gerrards Cross, Bucks, SL9 8SZ

Cover design by Alister MacInnes

Printed and bound by J.W Arrowsmith, Bristol

Unless otherwise stated, quotations from the Bible are from the New International Version, © 1973, 1978, 1984 by International Bible Society, published in Great Britain by Hodder and Stoughton Ltd.